ARCTIC
and
ANTARCTIC
REGIONS

Troll Associates

ARCTIC
and
ANTARCTIC
REGIONS

by Francene Sabin

Illustrated by Allan Eitzen

Troll Associates

Library of Congress Cataloging in Publication Data

Sabin, Francene.
    Arctic and Antarctic regions.

    Summary: Briefly describes the frozen regions around
the North Pole and the South Pole, which are alike in
many ways and different in many others.
    1. Polar regions—Juvenile literature. [1. Polar
regions. 2. Arctic regions. 3. Antarctic regions]
I. Eitzen, Allan, ill. II. Title.
G590.S2   1985   919.8   84-2730
ISBN 0-8167-0234-9 (lib. bdg.)
ISBN 0-8167-0235-7 (pbk.)

Icebergs float like crystal castles, hard as marble, smooth as glass, and white as milk. Walruses sun themselves on a rocky Alaskan beach. Pale yellow Arctic poppies bloom in the short summer of the frozen North. The powerful polar bear and the hardy reindeer move across endless seas of ice and snow. This is the Arctic.

Far, far away, a frozen continent lies beneath sheets of ice that are hundreds of feet thick. Here and there, bare, jagged mountains of rock jut up through the ice and snow. Crowds of penguins waddle to the icy water's edge, and vicious spotted leopard seals hunt smaller prey. This is the Antarctic.

The Arctic and Antarctic, at opposite ends of the Earth, are different in many ways and alike in many ways. Both have fascinated scientists and explorers for centuries. Both offer a challenge that has never lost its edge. And both still hold more mysteries than any other place in the world.

The Arctic and Antarctic are regions of extreme cold. In the center of each region is an imaginary pole.

The North Pole, in the Arctic, is the northernmost spot in the world. If you were to stand on that spot, every place around you would be south of where you are.

The South Pole, in the Antarctic, is the southernmost spot in the world. If you were to stand on that spot, every place around you would be north of where you are.

The North and South Poles are exactly opposite each other. The Earth's axis is an imaginary line that connects these two points as it runs through the center of the planet. The Earth spins on its axis. This spinning gives us day and night.

The Earth's axis is tilted, so the whole Earth is tilted at an angle. It is because of this angle that we have shorter days in one season and longer days in another season.

Where most people live the days vary in length by just a few hours. But in the polar regions there are six-month days and six-month nights. A polar summer day, however, is never really hot. And though it is light, it is not like midday all the time. For a short while during every twenty-four hours, the sun seems to set below the horizon. But it never does set completely.

The borderlines between these areas that have six-month days and six-month nights, and the rest of the world, are called the Arctic and Antarctic Circles. Inside the Arctic Circle lies the Arctic Ocean, most of Greenland, and parts of Alaska, Canada, Siberia, and Scandinavia.

The Arctic Ocean is not like oceans in warmer parts of the world because of the extreme cold. The permanent deep-freeze conditions have created thick ice that never melts. In the summer the ice cracks into huge floating islands and icebergs. In the winter the Arctic ice is almost one solid mass.

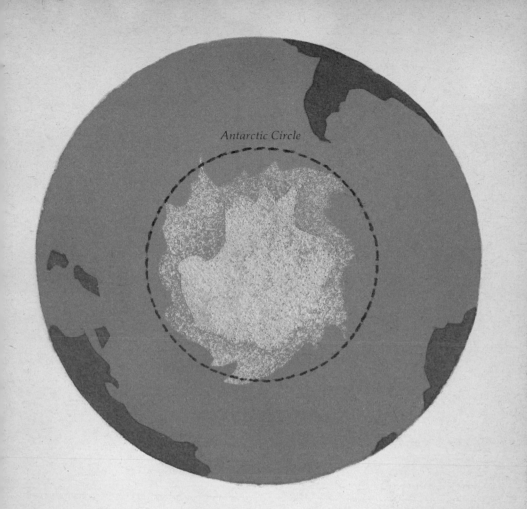

Almost all the area inside the Antarctic Circle is land covered by an enormous ice sheet. This land is the continent of Antarctica, which is larger than either Europe or Australia. But unlike all the other continents, Antarctica has no permanent population. It is regarded as international territory to be used for peaceful purposes only.

15

Twelve countries maintain scientific bases on this frozen continent. The researchers from these countries—which include the United States, the Soviet Union, Great Britain, and Japan—cooperate with each other in many ways. They share information, help each other in times of need, and even work together on a number of projects.

In addition to the Arctic and Antarctic Circles, there are other boundaries that separate the polar regions from the rest of the world. In the Arctic, the permafrost line acts as a natural boundary. Permafrost is land that is permanently frozen.

Permafrost is so hard that it seems to be as sturdy as rock. But it can be melted. When that happens, the ground shifts and becomes muddy and spongy.

When a house is built right on top of permafrost, the heat passes through the floor of the house and melts the permafrost. Then the building begins to sink. One of the ways to avoid this problem is to build Arctic houses above ground on wooden stilts, so that cold air passes between the house and the ground.

The Antarctic Convergence forms a different kind of natural boundary around the Antarctic Region. The Antarctic Convergence is the place where the Antarctic Ocean waters meet the waters of the Atlantic, Pacific, and Indian Oceans. Antarctic Ocean waters are colder and less salty than the waters of the other oceans.

The Antarctic Convergence is from twenty to thirty miles wide and circles the continent of Antarctica. It has a strong east-to-west current that follows the same path year after year. This area is rich in the tiny plant and animal life called plankton. There is so much plankton in the Antarctic Convergence that the water there is bright green and smells like freshly cut grass.

Even though the polar regions are cold, there is a noticeable difference between summer and winter temperatures. This is particularly true in the Arctic. The winter temperatures often drop to 60 degrees below zero Fahrenheit, or lower. But summer temperatures in certain areas may reach as high as 60 degrees above zero.

When summer comes, the thin layer of soil on top of the permafrost thaws. The ground becomes soft and spongy. Marsh grasses and mosses spring to life in this seasonal warmth.

Arctic plants are mostly very small, low-growing, and hardy. There are about nine hundred kinds of flowers, five hundred kinds of mosses, and two thousand kinds of lichens.

Reindeer

Musk ox

Lichens are slow-growing plants that are able to survive for long periods of time in extreme cold and without food. Lichens are an important part of the diet of Arctic animals. Reindeer, caribou, and musk oxen feed on the lichens and on any other plant life they can find.

When winter comes, these animals move south from the frozen tundra to places where they will find food. These places are south of the tree line. No trees grow on the tundra north of this line. The soil on top of the permafrost is not thick enough to hold tree roots, and the cold winds that whip over the tundra freeze and kill any new growth.

Caribou

In the summer the tundra is filled with life. There are ermine and Arctic hares, grizzly bears and foxes, lemmings and wolves, owls and ptarmigan, and dozens of other animals.

Grizzly bear

Wolf

Ptarmigan

Arctic hare

Owl

Ermine

Lemming

Walrus

Narwhal

Seal

But when winter returns, most of the animals move south or burrow into their nests in the ground. Few species remain active all year, though the seals, walruses, narwhals, and other ocean creatures do.

There are far fewer forms of life in the Antarctic than in the Arctic. Only three kinds of flowering plants, seventy-five kinds of mosses, and a few hundred kinds of lichens live on the continent of Antarctica. No large land mammals are found here. Even microscopic bacteria are scarce.

The dominant life form of Antarctica is the penguin. The penguin is a flightless bird whose wings have evolved into flippers. These paddle-like flippers, plus the bird's webbed feet, make the penguin an excellent swimmer.

Penguins and seals live along the coast of Antarctica and eat fish and a form of sea life called krill. Krill are small, shrimp-like creatures. Whales also visit the waters around Antarctica to feed on krill.

There are minerals on the continent of Antarctica, but they are not high-grade minerals, and they are too difficult to mine.

Antarctica's greatest importance lies in its value to the scientific community. Several research stations have been established where scientists are studying weather, magnetism, survival techniques, communication methods, as well as air pollution and space travel.

During the ice ages, much of the Earth was covered by snow and ice. When the tempera-

tures rose, the ice melted everywhere except in the polar regions. There, the bleak, chilling conditions remained.

But scientists have found fossils of plant life and deposits of coal—which forms from prehistoric plants—frozen in the Antarctic wasteland.

Was this frigid polar continent once a warm-weather land, covered with green plants and tall trees? Scientists believe that it was. But just when it became a frozen polar desert, no one knows. And no one knows what other secrets lie locked beneath the ice and snow in the Arctic and Antarctic permafrost.